The Homebuyers Handbook

Your field guide for finding, purchasing and maintaining a home

Shana O'Brien

DEDICATION

This book is dedicated to the pursuit of homeownership,
to all who pursue it and help make it happen.

TABLE OF CONTENTS

4 REASONS TO BUY A HOME THIS YEAR!

Here are four great reasons to consider buying a home today instead of waiting.

1. Prices Will Continue to Rise

CoreLogic's latest *Home Price Index* reports that home prices have appreciated by 6.3% over the last 12 months. The same report predicts that prices will continue to increase at a rate of 5.2% over the next year.

The bottom in home prices has come and gone. Home values will continue to appreciate for years. Waiting no longer makes sense.

2. Mortgage Interest Rates Are Projected to Increase

Freddie Mac's Primary Mortgage Market Survey shows that interest rates for a 30-year mortgage have remained around 4%. Most experts predict that they will begin to rise over the next 12 months. *The Mortgage Bankers Association, Fannie Mae, Freddie Mac & the National Association of Realtors* are in unison, projecting that rates will increase by this time next year.

An increase in rates will impact YOUR monthly mortgage payment. A year from now, your housing expense will increase if a mortgage is necessary to buy your next home.

3. Either Way You are Paying a Mortgage

As a paper from the *Joint Center for Housing Studies at Harvard University* explains:

> *"Households must consume housing whether they own or rent. Not even accounting for more favorable tax treatment of owning, homeowners pay debt service to pay down their own principal while households that rent pay down the principal of a landlord plus a rate of return. That's yet another reason owning often does—as Americans intuit— end up making more financial sense than renting."*

4. It's Time to Move On with Your Life

The 'cost' of a home is determined by two major components: the price of the home and the current mortgage rate. It appears that both are on the rise.

But what if they weren't? Would you wait?

Look at the actual reason you are buying and decide whether it is worth waiting. Whether you want to have a great place for your children to grow up, you want your family to be safer or you just want to have control over renovations, maybe now is the time to buy.

If the right thing for you and your family is to purchase a home this year, buying sooner rather than later could lead to substantial savings.

BUYING IS NOW 37.7% CHEAPER THAN RENTING IN THE US

The results of the latest *Rent vs. Buy Report* from *Trulia* show that homeownership remains cheaper than renting with a traditional 30-year fixed rate mortgage in the 100 largest metro areas in the United States.

The updated numbers actually show that the range is an average of 17.4% less expensive in Honolulu (HI), all the way up to 53.2% less expensive in Miami & West Palm Beach (FL), and 37.7% nationwide!

Other interesting findings in the report include:
- Interest rates have remained low, and even though home prices have appreciated around the country, they haven't greatly outpaced rental appreciation.
- Home prices would have to appreciate by a range of over 23% in Honolulu (HI), up to over 45% in Ventura County (CA), to reach the tipping point of renting being less expensive than buying.
- Nationally, rates would have to reach 9.1%, a 145% increase over today's average of 3.7%, for renting to be cheaper than buying. Rates haven't been that high since January of 1995, according to *Freddie Mac*.

Bottom Line
Buying a home makes sense socially and financially. If you are one of the many renters out there who would like to evaluate your ability to buy this year, let's get together to find your dream home.

HOME PRICES OVER THE LAST YEAR

Every quarter, the *Federal Housing Finance Agency (FHFA)* reports on the year-over-year changes in home prices. Below, you will see that prices are up year-over-year in every region.

Year-over-Year Prices Regionally

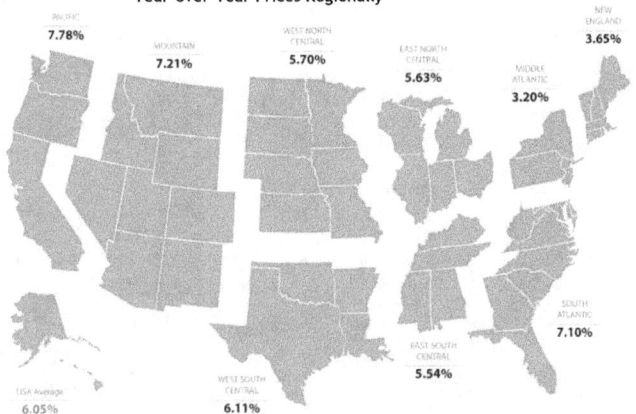

Looking at the breakdown by state, you can see that each state is appreciating at a different rate. This is important to know if you are planning on relocating to a different area of the country. Waiting to move may end up costing you more!

Year-over-Year Prices By State

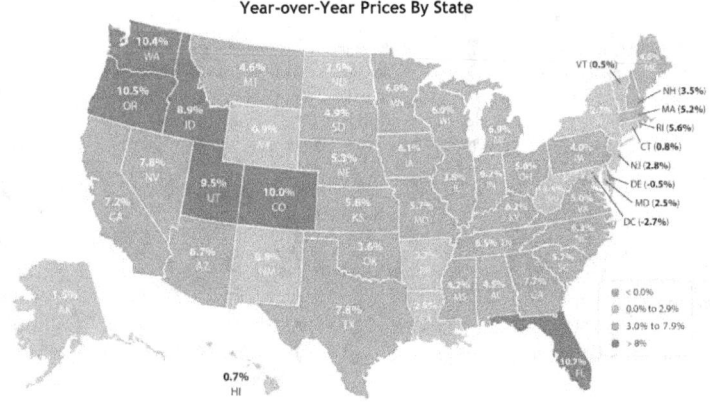

BUYING A HOME?
CONSIDER COST NOT JUST PRICE

As a seller, you will be most concerned about 'short term price' – where home values are headed over the next six months. As a buyer, however, you must not be concerned about price, but instead about the 'long term cost' of the home.

The *Mortgage Bankers Association (MBA)*, the *National Association of Realtors (NAR)* and *Freddie Mac* all project that mortgage interest rates will increase by this time next year. According to *CoreLogic's* most recent *Home Price Index Report*, home prices will appreciate by 5.2% over the next 12 months.

What Does This Mean as a Buyer?

Here is a simple demonstration of the impact an interest rate increase would have on the mortgage payment of a home selling for approximately $250,000 today if home prices appreciate by the 5.2% predicted by *CoreLogic* <u>over the next twelve months</u>:

	Mortgage	Interest Rate	Payment (P&I)
Today	$250,000	4.00%	**$1,193.54**
Q4 2017	$263,250	4.20%	**$1,286.12**
Difference in Monthly Payment			**$92.58**

*Rates based on Freddie Mac's prediction at time of print

Monthly	Annually	Over 30 Years
$92.58	$1,110.96	$33,329

The Cost of
RENTING vs. BUYING

HISTORICALLY:	NOW:

Percentage of Income Needed to Afford Median Rent

26%	30%

Percentage of Income Needed to Afford a Median Home

21%	15%

If you are renting & think you can't afford a home... THINK AGAIN!

*BUYING COSTS **SIGNIFICANTLY LESS** THAN RENTING!*

Either way you're paying a mortgage, why not have it be YOURS?

Source: Pulsenomics

STARTING TO LOOK FOR A HOME? KNOW WHAT YOU WANT VS. WHAT YOU NEED

In this day and age of being able to shop for anything anywhere, it is really important to know what you're looking for when you start your home search.

If you've been thinking about buying a home of your own for some time now, you've probably come up with a list of things that you'd LOVE to have in your new home. Many new homebuyers fantasize about the amenities that they see on television or *Pinterest*, and start looking at the countless homes listed for sale with rose-colored glasses.

Do you really need that farmhouse sink in the kitchen in order to be happy with your home choice? Would a two-car garage be a convenience or a necessity? Could the man cave of your dreams be a future renovation project instead of a make or break now?

The first step in your home buying process should be to get pre-approved for your mortgage. This allows you to know your budget before you fall in love with a home that is way outside of it.

The next step is to list all the features of a home that you would like & to qualify them as follows:

- **'Must Haves'** – if this property does not have these items, then it shouldn't even be considered. *(ex: distance from work or family, number of bedrooms/bathrooms)*
- **'Should Haves'** – if the property hits all of the must haves and some of the should haves, it stays in contention, but does not *need* to have all of these features.
- **'Absolute Wish List'** – if we find a property in our budget that has all of the 'must haves,' most of the 'should haves,' and ANY of these, it's the winner!

Bottom Line
Having this list flushed out before starting your search will save you time and frustration, while also letting your agent know what features are most important to you before starting to show you houses in your desired area.

YOU NEED A PROFESSIONAL WHEN BUYING A HOME

Many people wonder whether they should hire a real estate professional to assist them in buying their dream home or if they should first try to do it on their own. In today's market: you need an experienced professional!

You Need an Expert Guide if You Are Traveling a Dangerous Path

The field of real estate is loaded with land mines. You need a true expert to guide you through the dangerous pitfalls that currently exist. Finding a home that is priced appropriately and ready for you to move in to can be tricky. An agent listens to your wants and needs, and can sift out the homes that do not fit within the parameters of your "dream home."

You Need a Skilled Negotiator

In today's market, hiring a talented negotiator could save you thousands, perhaps tens of thousands of dollars. Each step of the way – from the original offer, to the possible renegotiation of that offer after a home inspection, to the possible cancellation of the deal based on a troubled appraisal – you need someone who can keep the deal together until it closes.

Realize that when an agent is negotiating their commission with you, they are negotiating their own salary; the salary that keeps a roof over their family's head; the salary that puts food on their family's table. If they are quick to take less when negotiating for themselves and their families, what makes you think they will not act the same way when negotiating for you and your family? If they were Clark Kent when negotiating with you, they will not turn into Superman when negotiating with the buyer or seller in your deal.

Bottom Line

Famous sayings become famous because they are true. You get what you pay for. Just like a good accountant or a good attorney, a good agent will save you money…not cost you money.

WHAT DO YOU ACTUALLY NEED TO QUALIFY FOR A MORTGAGE?

Fannie Mae's "What Do Consumers Know About The Mortgage Qualification Criteria?" Study revealed that Americans are misinformed about what is really required to qualify for a mortgage when purchasing a home.

To help correct these misunderstandings, let's take a look at the survey results compared to the latest *Ellie Mae Origination Insight Report,* which focuses on recently approved loans.

Survey Results vs. What's Really Required

59% of Americans either don't know (54%) or are misinformed (5%) about what FICO score is necessary to qualify.

Many Americans believe a 'good' credit score is 780 or higher. 53.9% of approved mortgages had a credit score of 600-749.

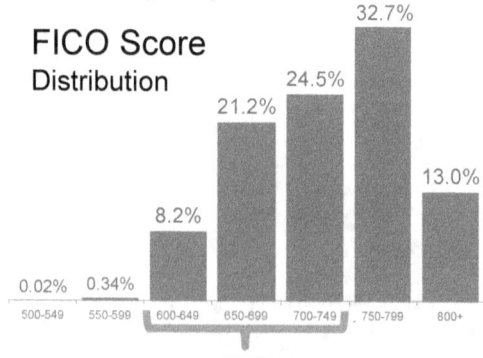

FICO Score
Distribution

500-549	550-599	600-649	650-699	700-749	750-799	800+
0.02%	0.34%	8.2%	21.2%	24.5%	32.7%	13.0%

53.9%

76% of Americans either don't know (40%) or are misinformed (36%) about the minimum down payment required.

Many believe that they need at least 20% down to buy their dream home. New programs actually let buyers put down as little as 3%.

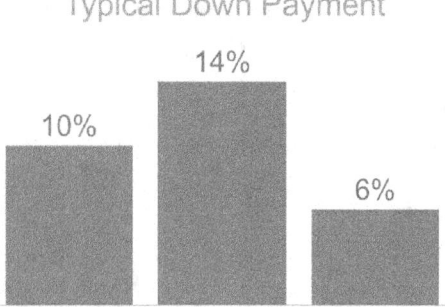

Typical Down Payment

- All Buyers: 10%
- Repeat Buyers: 14%
- 1st Time Buyers: 6%

Bottom Line

Whether buying your first home or moving up to your dream home, knowing your options will definitely make the mortgage process easier. Your dream home may already be within your reach.

YOU CAN SAVE FOR A DOWN PAYMENT FASTER THAN YOU THINK

In a study conducted by *Builder.com*, researchers determined that nationwide, it would take *"nearly eight years"* for a first-time buyer to save enough for a down payment on their dream home.

Depending on where you live, median rents, incomes and home prices all vary. By determining the percentage of income a renter spends on housing in each state, and the amount needed for a 10% down payment, they were able to establish how long (in years) it would take for an average resident to save.

According to the study, residents in South Dakota are able to save for a down payment the quickest in just under 3.5 years.

On the right is a map created using the data for each state.

What if you only needed to save 3%?

What if you were able to take advantage of one of the *Freddie Mac* or *Fannie Mae* 3% down programs?

Suddenly saving for a down payment no longer takes 5 or 10 years, but becomes attainable in under two years in many states *(as shown in the map on the right)*.

Bottom Line

Whether you have just started to save for a down payment, or have been for years, you may be closer to your dream home than you think!

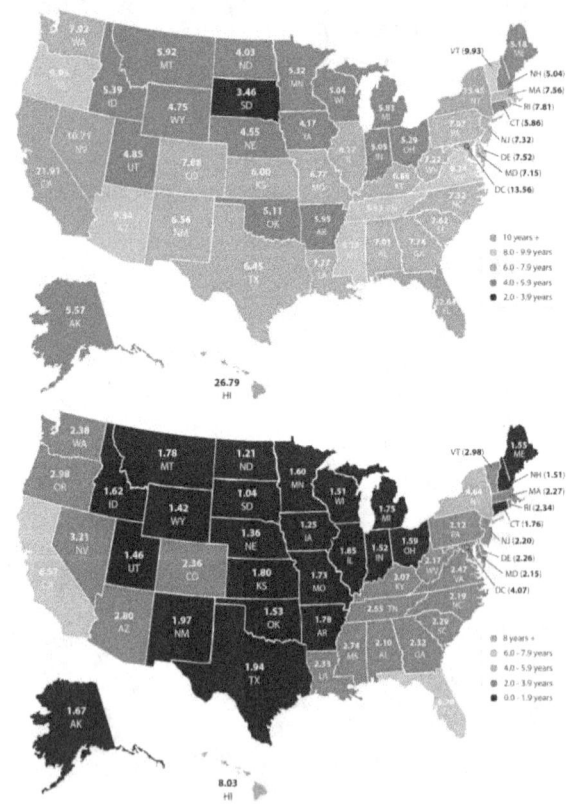

13

WHY GETTING PRE-APPROVED SHOULD BE YOUR FIRST STEP

In many markets across the country, the amount of buyers searching for their dream home greatly outnumbers the amount of homes for sale. This has led to a competitive marketplace where buyers often need to stand out. One way to show you are serious about buying your dream home is to get pre-qualified or pre-approved for a mortgage before starting your search.

But even if you are in a market that is not as competitive, knowing your budget will give you the confidence to know if your dream home is within your reach.

Freddie Mac lays out the advantages of pre-approval in the 'My Home' section of their website.

> *"It's highly recommended that you work with your lender to get pre-approved before you begin house hunting. Pre-approval will tell you how much home you can afford and can help you move faster, and with greater confidence, in competitive markets."*

One of the many advantages of working with a local real estate professional is that many have relationships with lenders who will be able to help you with this process. Once you have selected a lender, you will need to fill out their loan application and provide them with important information regarding *"your credit, debt, work history, down payment and residential history."*

Freddie Mac describes the 4 Cs that help determine the amount you will be qualified to borrow:

- **Capacity:** Your current and future ability to make your payments
- **Capital or cash reserves:** The money, savings and investments you have that can be sold quickly for cash
- **Collateral:** The home, or type of home, that you would like to purchase
- **Credit:** Your history of paying bills and other debts on time

Getting pre-approved is one of many steps that will show home sellers that you are serious about buying and it often helps speed up the process once your offer has been accepted.

Bottom Line
Many potential home buyers overestimate the down payment and credit scores needed to qualify for a mortgage today. If you are ready and willing to buy, you may be pleasantly surprised at your ability to do so as well.

What You Need to Know About The
MORTGAGE PROCESS

What You'll Need to Qualify in Today's Market:

✓ **Downpayment:**
Generally between 5-20% of the purchase price *(40% of buyers are putting down less than 10% - with many putting down as little as 3%)*

✓ **Income Verification, Credit History & Asset Documentation**

✓ **Impartial Third-Party Appraisal:**
Your lender needs this to verify the value of the house you want to purchase.

✓ **Stable Income** ✓ **Good Credit History**

You will interact with various **professionals** during the home buying process, all of whom are **valuable resources** & perform **necessary roles**.

Steps To Take:

Find out your current credit history & score.
You don't want to start out with any surprises.

Start gathering all of your documentation:
Income Verification (W-2 forms, tax returns, employment), Credit History & Assets (such as bank statements to verify your savings)

Contact a professional to help you develop a spending plan & determine how much you can afford.

Consult with your lender to review your income, expenses & financial goals to determine the type and amount of mortgage you qualify for.

Talk to your lender about applying for a mortgage & getting a pre-approval letter. This letter provides an estimate of what you might be able to borrow *(provided your financial status doesn't change)* & demonstrates to home sellers that you are a serious buyer.

Bottom Line:
Do your research, reach out to the professionals, stick to your budget & be sure you are ready to take on the financial responsibilities of being a homeowner.

GETTING A MORTGAGE: WHY SO MUCH PAPERWORK?

Why is there so much paperwork mandated by lenders for a mortgage loan application when buying a home today? It seems that they need to know everything about you and require three separate sources to validate each and every entry on the application form.

Many buyers are being told by friends and family that the process was a hundred times easier when they bought their home ten to twenty years ago.

There are two very good reasons that the loan process is much more onerous on today's buyer than perhaps any time in history.

1. The government has set new guidelines that now demand that the bank prove beyond any doubt that you are indeed capable of paying the mortgage.

During the run-up in the housing market, many people 'qualified' for mortgages that they could never pay back. This led to millions of families losing their homes. The government wants to make sure this can't happen again.

2. The banks don't want to be in the real estate business.

Over the last seven years, banks were forced to take on the responsibility of liquidating millions of foreclosures and also negotiating another million+ short sales. Just like the government, they don't want more foreclosures. For that reason, they need to double (maybe even triple) check everything on the application.

However, there is some good news about this situation.

The housing crash that mandated that banks be extremely strict on paperwork requirements also allowed you to get a mortgage interest rate around 4%.

The friends and family who bought homes ten or twenty years ago experienced a simpler mortgage application process but also paid a higher interest rate (the average 30-year fixed rate mortgage was 8.12% in the 1990s and 6.29% in the 2000s).

If you went to the bank and offered to pay 7% instead of around 4%, they would probably bend over backwards to make the process much easier.

Bottom Line

Instead of concentrating on the additional paperwork required, let's be thankful that we are able to buy a home at historically low rates.

READY TO MAKE AN OFFER? 4 TIPS FOR SUCCESS

So you've been searching for that perfect house to call a 'home' and you finally found one! The price is right, and in such a competitive market you want to make sure you make a good offer so that you can guarantee your dream of making this house yours comes true!

Freddie Mac covered *"4 Tips for Making an Offer"* in their latest *Executive Perspective.* Here are the 4 tips they covered along with some additional information for your consideration:

1. Understand How Much You Can Afford

> *"While it's not nearly as fun as house hunting, fully understanding your finances is critical in making an offer."*

This 'tip' or 'step' really should take place before you start your home search process.

Getting pre-approved is one of many steps that will show home sellers that you are serious about buying, and will allow you to make your offer with the confidence of knowing that you have already been approved for a mortgage for that amount. You will also need to know if you are prepared to make any repairs that may need to be made to the house (ex: new roof, new furnace).

2. Act Fast

> *"Even though there are fewer investors, the inventory of homes for sale is also low and competition for housing continues to heat up in many parts of the country."*

The inventory of homes listed for sale has remained well below the 6-month supply that is needed for a 'normal' market. Buyer demand has continued to outpace the supply of homes for sale, causing buyers to compete with each other for their dream home.

Make sure that as soon as you decide that you want to make an offer, you work with your agent to present it as soon as possible.

3. Make a Solid Offer

Freddie Mac offers this advice to help make your offer the strongest it can be:

> *"Your strongest offer will be comparable with other sales and listings in the neighborhood. A licensed real estate agent active in the neighborhoods you are considering will be instrumental in helping you put in a solid offer based on their experience and other key considerations such as recent sales of similar homes, the condition of the house and what you can afford."*

Consider ways of making your offer stand out! Many buyers write a personal letter to the seller letting them know how much they would love to be the new homeowners. Your agent will be able to help you figure out if there are any other ways your offer could stand above the rest.

4. Be Prepared to Negotiate

> *"It's likely that you'll get at least one counteroffer from the sellers so be prepared. The two things most likely to be negotiated are the selling price and closing date. Given that, you'll be glad you did your homework first to understand how much you can afford.*
>
> *Your agent will also be key in the negotiation process, giving you guidance on the counteroffer and making sure that the agreed-to contract terms are met."*

If your offer is approved, *Freddie Mac* urges you to *"always get an independent home inspection, so you know the true condition of the home. If the inspection uncovers undisclosed problems or issues, you can typically re-negotiate the terms or cancel the contract."*

Bottom Line
Whether buying your first home or your fifth, having a local real estate professional who is an expert in their market on your side is your best bet to make sure the process goes smoothly. Let's talk about how we can make your dreams of homeownership a reality!

WHAT TO EXPECT WHEN HOME INSPECTING

So you made an offer, it was accepted, and now your next task is to have the home inspected prior to closing. More often than not, your agent may have made your offer contingent on a clean home inspection.

This contingency allows you to renegotiate the price paid for the home, ask the sellers to cover repairs, or even, in some cases, walk away. Your agent can advise you on the best course of action once the report is filed.

How to Choose an Inspector

Your agent will most likely have a short list of inspectors that they have worked with in the past that they can recommend to you. *Realtor.com* suggests that you consider the following 5 areas when choosing the right home inspector for you:

- **Qualifications** - find out what's included in your inspection & if the age or location of your home may warrant specific certifications or specialties.
- **Sample Reports** - ask for a sample inspection report so you can review how thoroughly they will be inspecting your dream home. The more detailed the report the better in most cases.
- **References** - do your homework - ask for phone numbers and names of past clients that you can call to ask about their experience.
- **Memberships** - Not all inspectors belong to a national or state association of home inspectors, and membership in one of these groups should not be the only way to evaluate your choice. Often membership in one of these organizations means that there is continued training and education provided.
- **Errors & Omission Insurance** - Find out what the liability of the inspector or inspection company is once the inspection is over. The inspector is only human after all, and it is possible that they might miss something they should have seen.

Ask your inspector if it's ok for you to tag along during the inspection. That way they can point out anything that should be addressed or fixed.

Don't be surprised to see your inspector climbing on the roof, crawling around in the attic, and on the floors. The job of the inspector is to protect your investment and find any issues with the home, including but not limited to: the roof, plumbing, electrical components, appliances, heating & air conditioning systems, ventilation, windows, the fireplace & chimney, the foundation & so much more!

Bottom Line

They say 'ignorance is bliss,' but not when investing your hard-earned money in a home of your own. Work with a professional you can trust to give you the most information possible about your new home so that you can make the most educated decision about your purchase.

HAVE YOU PUT ASIDE ENOUGH FOR CLOSING COSTS?

There are many potential homebuyers, and even sellers, who believe that you need at least a 20% down payment in order to buy a home, or move on to their next home. Time after time, we have dispelled this myth by showing that there are many loan programs that allow you to put down as little as 3% (or 0% with a VA loan).

If you have saved up your down payment and are ready to start your home search, one other piece of the puzzle is to make sure that you have saved enough for your closing costs.

Freddie Mac defines closing costs as:

> *"Closing costs, also called settlement fees, will need to be paid when you obtain a mortgage. These are fees charged by people representing your purchase, including your lender, real estate agent, and other third parties involved in the transaction.*
>
> **Closing costs are typically between 2 and 5% of your purchase price."**

We've recently heard from many first-time homebuyers that they wished that someone had let them know that closing costs could be so high. If you think about it, with a low down payment program, your closing costs could equal the amount that you saved for your down payment.

Here is a list of just some of the fees/costs that may be included in your closing costs, depending on where the home you wish to purchase is located:

- Government recording costs
- Appraisal fees
- Credit report fees
- Lender origination fees
- Title services (insurance, search fees)
- Tax service fees
- Survey fees
- Attorney fees
- Underwriting fees

Is there any way to avoid paying closing costs?

Work with your lender and real estate agent to see if there are any ways to decrease or defer your closing costs. There are no-closing mortgages available, but they end up costing you more in the end with a higher interest rate, or by wrapping the closing costs into the total cost of the mortgage *(meaning you'll end up paying interest on your closing costs)*.

Home buyers can also negotiate with the seller over who pays these fees. Sometimes the seller will agree to assume the buyer's closing fees in order to get the deal finalized.

Bottom Line

Speak with your lender and agent early and often to determine how much you'll be responsible for at closing. Finding out you'll need to come up with thousands of dollars right before closing is not a surprise anyone is ever looking forward to.

CONTACT ME TO TALK MORE

I'm sure you have questions and concerns…

I would love to talk with you more about what you read here, and help you on the path to buying a home. My contact information is below. I look forward to hearing from you…

Shana O'Brien, REALTOR®
Berkshire Hathaway Home Services
NW Real Estate
www.ShanaOBrien.com